How to Play Drums

by JOEL ROTHMAN

Illustrated by Jerry Warshaw

ALBERT WHITMAN & Company, Chicago

The Music Involvement Series

Library of Congress Cataloging in Publication Data

Rothman, Joel.
  How to play drums.

  SUMMARY: A guide to drum playing that includes
exercises and techniques to practice and master.
    1. Drums—Methods—Juvenile.   [1. Drum—Methods]
I. Warshaw, Jerry.   II. Title.
MT801.D7R7   789'.1   76-39937
ISBN 0-8075-3420-X

Text © 1977 by Joel Rothman
Illustrations © 1977 by Albert Whitman & Company
Published simultaneously in Canada by
George J. McLeod, Limited, Ontario

Contents

DO YOU WANT TO BE A DRUMMER?

Many types of music require a drummer—jazz, rock, Latin, symphonic, and dance music. Certain styles of music call for different skills. For example, a drummer who plays in a symphony orchestra must read music well and be able to follow the conductor. To play jazz, drummers are expected to be creative. Often at a moment's notice they are asked to improvise or play solos.

The main work of a drummer in a dance band or rock group is to supply a solid, steady beat, in other words, to keep time. The drummer must be able to play a particular rhythm without speeding up or slowing down. In a sense, the drummer acts as the clock for the band.

The skills needed to play jazz and symphonic music come after many years of study. But playing with a small dance band or rock group does not always require a wide musical background. You don't need great speed and control with the drumsticks or a thorough knowledge of how to read music to begin playing. Of course this does not mean that professional drummers with small dance bands or rock groups cannot improvise, play solos, and read music. It only means that these skills do not have to be highly developed when you play on an elementary level as an amateur in a small group with friends.

Drums are special because they're one of the few instruments you can begin to learn on your own. In the early stages, you are most concerned with learning very simple rhythms. Other instrumentalists must master rhythm, too. But they also have to learn to read notes with different pitches, as well as how to finger these notes correctly. They must produce a good tone and play in tune, not sharp or flat. Most of this is of no concern to a drummer, at least not at first.

I am not trying to make the study of drums seem easier than it is. There are, in fact, several elements in drumming that are awkward and unnatural, yet have to be overcome. This is especially true when playing one pattern with your hands and a different one with your feet. But in the beginning, at least, drums are far less difficult to learn than other instruments.

This book shows you the most basic beats and how to play them at a set of drums. As you'll see, you don't even have to own a set of drums to get started. The exercises are simple enough so that you can understand them and play them without the help of a teacher. You can begin drumming on your own.

This is a practical book, designed for self-teaching. But it can only take you so far. How much more you want to learn will depend upon you. If after mastering the exercises here your interest in drums is strong, you may seek a teacher to obtain professional training. How to find a teacher is discussed at the end of this book. Meanwhile, if you practice the exercises on the next pages you should be able to play drums in an amateur dance band or rock group. You'll be playing on a very elementary level, it's true, but you'll be a drummer!

GETTING READY

You may think that when you study drums you learn right at the instrument. That's what you do with piano, clarinet, flute, or guitar. But beginning to play drums is different. Many students learn to play on a practice pad, not at the actual set of drums. In fact, a drum set isn't even going to be talked about in this book until later.

The practice pad is a flat piece of rubber glued to a block of wood. It gives the feel of playing a drum, but not the sound. Pads come in different sizes. Some are mounted on adjustable stands. For the first year, at least, most of your practice time is spent using a pad.

You can buy a practice pad. Its cost will depend upon the quality. Some are less than ten dollars, others are much more. But before you buy a pad, why not make your own? It will be good enough for the time being.

Find a block of wood about five or six inches square and an inch or so thick.

What can you use for the rubber? A piece cut from the sole of an old sneaker will do very well. Glue the rubber to the block of wood, and presto! you have a practice pad.

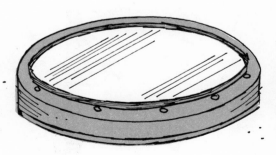 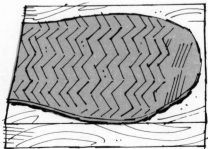

Your family and neighbors will be happy that most of your practice time will be at the pad. Since you don't play sweet melodies on drums, listening as you beat out rhythm several hours a day could make you pretty unpopular with many people.

You Want to Start Now? Here's What to Do

Without a practice pad or even drumsticks, you can begin right now. Simply sit down, get comfortable, and tap the exercises on your thighs. Does that sound easy? It is!

This is a good way to begin because drums are a rather expensive instrument. While many people feel they want to learn how to play, they often lose interest in a short time. So before you think about buying drums, practice the exercises in the first two chapters on your thighs. After that, you will be introduced to the different parts of the drum set and how to play them. It will be time then to explore the possibility of getting a set of drums.

UNDERSTANDING QUARTER-NOTES AND EIGHTH-NOTES

For the basic beats in this book you'll need to read quarter-notes and eighth-notes. If you concentrate, you can learn to play the exercises in this section within a few minutes—an hour at most.

If you have trouble, ask someone who plays an instrument for help. Anyone who has studied an instrument for even a few weeks will understand what is being presented.

Remember: I'm assuming that you do not have a drum set, a drum pad, or drumsticks. And even if you do, simply have a seat and tap the rhythm in the following exercises with your right hand on your right thigh.

I'll also assume that you are right-handed, but if you are not, you will use your *left* hand where I say *right,* and your *right* for *left.* Almost no other instrument gives the musician a choice in playing with his favorite or stronger hand. The piano, for instance, is built one way, and whether you are right-handed or left-handed, you play the piano with the instrument facing you, your right hand playing the upper notes, and your left hand the lower notes. The drums, however, let you play lefty if you're a natural southpaw.

Meet the Quarter-Note

The head of a **quarter-note** looks like a large black dot. Fastened to the head is a thin stem, which may go up or down.

For now, all the exercises you will play have notes with their stems facing up.

Tap the following four quarter-notes with your right hand on your right thigh (or your left hand on your left thigh if you are left-handed). Count as you play
1, 2, 3, 4

EXERCISE 1

Count: **1   2   3   4**

Congratulations! You have just played one full **measure** of music.

In Exercise 2 you will tap the four quarter-notes two times. In other words, you will strike eight notes, one after each other. Try to play the notes evenly, without accenting one note more than another.

EXERCISE 2

Count: **1 2 3 4 1 2 3 4**

You have just played two measures of music. The different measures are always separated by thin lines called **bar lines.**

The next exercise again contains quarter-notes. This time, however, there are four measures. You will be playing sixteen consecutive notes.

EXERCISE 3
Count:　　　1　2　3　4　　　1　2　3　4　　　1　2　3　4　　　1　2　3　4

Excellent! as far as I can tell . . .

This is *important:* While playing from one measure to the next be sure that you keep a steady tempo. Do not speed up or slow down. Think of the second hand of a clock ticking away. It never pauses or hesitates, or if it does, it's time to get a new clock.

Now Meet the Eighth-Note

An **eighth-note** looks just like a quarter-note, but it has a flag hanging from the tip of its stem.

In arithmetic, two eighths equal a quarter (1/8 + 1/8 = 1/4). So it is in music, too: two eighth-notes equal a quarter-note.

12

Most of the time when you see groups of eighth-notes, they will be connected or beamed instead of having their own individual flags.

Tap the following exercise with your right hand on your right thigh. The two eighth-notes will have to be played twice as fast as the quarter-notes.

EXERCISE 4

Read the plus sign over the second eighth-note as "an." Keep repeating the exercise until you can play it without hesitation.

Exercise 5 contains four measures of quarter-notes and eighth-notes. Count out loud and move without a pause from playing one measure to the next.

EXERCISE 5

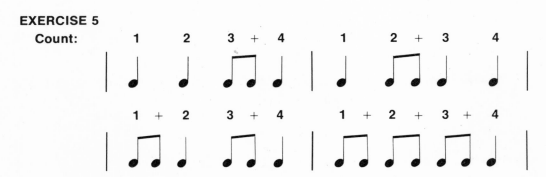

Try to practice this exercise for at least ten to fifteen minutes. Even if you feel you know it after only five minutes, continue to go over the rhythm so that it can be played more rapidly.

MOVING ON

You have been taught quarter-notes and eighth-notes. You have played rhythmic patterns based on these notes. They will make it possible for you to learn six of the basic beats for playing with a band. These beats are the Lindy or Jazz, Fox-trot, Waltz, Cha-cha, Rhumba, and Basic Rock beat.

You can learn these beats without having a set of drums. Continue to tap the exercises on your thighs. What you are going to do now is different because you will be tapping one pattern with your left hand on your left thigh while your right hand continues to tap on your right thigh.

You are also going to learn to use your feet. In other words, you will learn to use hands and feet and coordinate them to play the basic beats.

the ROCK

the LINDY

the WALTZ

The Lindy, or Jazz, Beat

Tap the four quarter-notes in the next exercise on your right thigh with your right hand. Keep repeating the exercise—that's easy enough.

In the next exercise there are two circled notes, like this: Tap the circled notes on your left thigh with your left hand. Now your right hand taps **1, 2, 3, 4** on your right thigh while your left hand taps the circled notes on the counts of 2 and 4 on your left thigh.

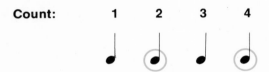

Keep repeating this exercise without hesitation until you can play it with smoothness and ease. Remember to keep your quarter-notes even.

You have mastered what your hands do in the jazz beat. Now you are going to tap with your right foot. This will take a certain amount of coordination, but it isn't very difficult. Your right foot will tap the same thing as your right hand: consecutive quarter-notes. Your right hand and your right foot will both be tapping **1, 2, 3, 4** at the same time. Your left hand will tap only on the counts of **2** and **4,** the circled notes.

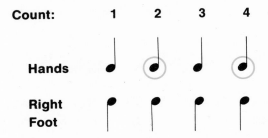

Notice that the notes for the right foot are shown with their stems facing down.

Repeat this exercise until you play it without any hesitation.

Ready for the final step? Here it is.

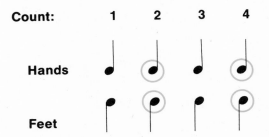

This time, you tap your left foot on the same count with your left hand. The right hand and the right foot play together on the counts **1, 2, 3, 4.** The left hand and the left foot play at the same time on the counts of **2** and **4,** but not on **1** or **3.** On counts of **2** and **4** both hands and both feet all play together.

So that's all there is to it. If you can do what has just been explained, you will be playing a simplified version of the basic Lindy or jazz beat. By practicing the exercise over and over, you should be able to master this beat within an hour or less. Don't try to play too quickly at first. Start slowly, and as you become comfortable with the coordination of hands and feet you can build up speed.

This same beat can also be used for the Fox-trot, which is a slower dance than the Lindy.

Perhaps the names "Lindy" and "Fox-trot" are ones you don't recognize. They are common ballroom dances—the Fox-trot has been danced for more than sixty years in the United States; the Lindy has been popular since the late 1920s. Although you may not be familiar with the names of these two dances, the beats for them are very useful to know.

The Rock Beat

Are you ready to learn a beat you'll use often? In the first exercise you will tap continuous eighth-notes with your right hand. Be sure to count as you play **"1 an, 2 an, 3 an, 4 an."** Keep repeating the rhythm without hesitating.

Two notes are circled in the next exercise. These notes will be played with the left hand while the right hand continues to tap eighth-notes.

Notice that the notes for the left hand fall on the counts of 2 and 4, just as they did in the Lindy beat. The one difference, of course, is that in the Lindy the right hand tapped quarter-notes; in the Rock beat, the right hand taps eighth-notes.

Tap both hands together on **2** and **4**.

It is time to add the right foot. The following exercise shows where the foot must play. Once again, as in the Lindy, the foot taps steady quarter-notes. This isn't really very difficult, but you must learn to play the exercise without the slightest bit of hesitation. It must become second nature, a habit, because there is no room for mistakes when you play the beat with a band.

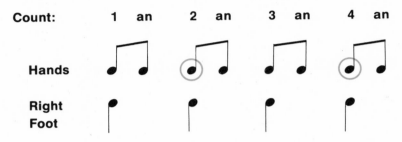

The final exercise, like the Lindy beat, includes the use of the left foot on the counts of 2 and 4. The left foot plays with the left hand.

Look at the exercise above. Replay it, but try to add your left foot together with your left hand.

I should make it clear that it is not essential to play your left foot. You can, if you have to, play in a band and never use your left foot. For our purposes, it would be enough to play with only your right hand, right foot, and left hand. The left foot, however, is usually used. So if you can coordinate it with the other parts, you should make use of your left foot.

When you have mastered this last beat you will be able to play the Cha-cha and Rhumba, as well as the basic Rock rhythm. Except for small differences, the same beat is used for each dance.

The Waltz

Here is a beat that is easy. The Waltz is a dance which is played in 3/4 time. In other words, instead of counting **1,   2,   3,   4,** you count **1,   2,   3;   1,   2,   3.**

For the Waltz, both feet tap together on the count of 1, then both hands tap together on the counts of 2 and 3.

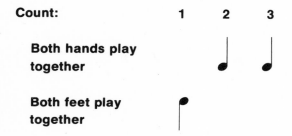

Be careful that you tap your feet only on the count of 1, not on 2 and 3.

Be careful to tap your hands only on 2 and 3, not on 1. Repeat this exercise until you can play it smoothly.

When you have mastered this exercise for the Waltz you will be able to play six basic beats at the drums: the Lindy, Fox-trot, Rhumba, Cha-cha, Rock beat, and Waltz. These six beats will let you play more than three-fourths of the music of most dance bands. In fact, the Rock beat will probably be the one you will find yourself using most of the time.

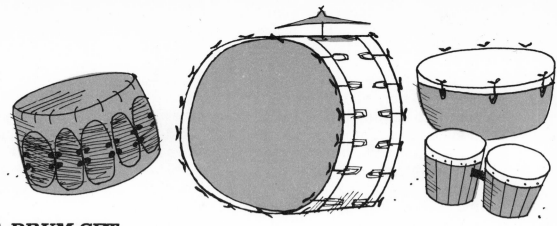

A DRUM SET

You have been learning the basic beats without ever sitting down at a drum set! Perhaps you've been practicing with the drum pad that you made or just by tapping on your thighs with your hands and on the floor with your feet. I think that if you have been serious in practicing and are able to play the different beats smoothly and without hesitation you're ready for the next step.

If you wish to continue, you will need an actual set of drums. If you do not have a set, my advice is to begin by renting one through your local music dealer. I do not recommend that you buy a set at this point.

Even though you have come this far, you may still lose interest in playing. Renting a set gives you a chance to decide whether or not you want to continue drumming without tying up a lot of money purchasing drums—should you decide to stop playing.

19

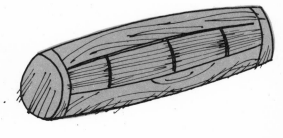

Some dealers will allow the first two or three months of rental fees to be counted toward the cost of the instrument should you decide to buy. In other words, if a set costs $500, and you rent it for $25 a month for three months, then you will be credited with $75 when you purchase. This is only an example, and you will have to explore costs at the time when you are ready to buy. It may be worth asking your dealer whether he has a used set which is in good condition and less costly than a new one.

There is a second reason to rent at this point. You may decide to find a teacher so that you can continue a more formal course of study. A teacher will then be able to help you with choosing a drum set. As a professional, your teacher has had experience and should know precisely how to guide you in your choice and where to buy at the best possible price.

There are listings of instruments for sale in newspapers and special publications. It is often quite possible to get a good buy if you know what to look for. But it is also possible to lose money. Unless you have someone with you who knows the value of used drums and what to look for, I suggest dealing with a local music store rather than an individual whose advertisement you have seen.

There are, in fact, music stores devoted exclusively to selling percussion instruments and related products. They can be found in a classified telephone directory. I have found that the people who own these specialized shops are usually professional drummers who have opened a business related to their field of interest. They generally have more expertise with drums than other music dealers and you may do well to rent or buy from them.

MEET THE DRUM SET

The most basic parts of a drum set are shown here. Such a set consists of snare drum, tom-tom, floor tom-tom, bass drum, ride cymbal, and hi-hat cymbals. Each of these will be described for you in the next pages.

The snare drum, tom-tom, floor tom-tom, and ride cymbal are played with the hands. The bass drum and hi-hat are played with the feet.

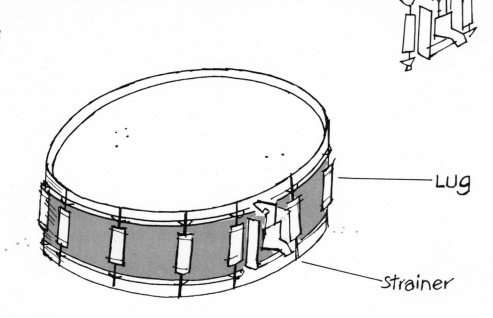

Lug

Strainer

The Snare Drum

The snare drum is really two drums in one because it can be made to produce two different sounds.

A set of **strainers (snares)** is attached to the bottom of the drum. A special switch on the side of the drum can bring the strainers tight against the bottom skin (head) or loosen them. When the strainers are tight against the bottom skin while the top skin is played upon, the vibrations cause the snare drum to produce its distinctive snare sound.

When the strainers are switched off and do not touch the bottom skin, the snare drum will sound like a high-pitched tom-tom.

You will be using both the snare sound and the tom-tom sound in learning to play certain beats. When I want the snare sound, I will ask for "Snares on," and when I want the tom-tom sound I will ask for "Snares off."

Notice that the bottom skin, or membrane, of the snare drum is thinner than the top skin, the one on which you play. This is because the skin you play upon must be stronger to withstand the pounding from sticks. The thinner skin on the bottom is also necessary because it is more sensitive to the vibrations of the strainers.

You can tighten or loosen the drum skins with a special key which is fitted to the lug heads on the sides of the snare drum. This key fits a four-sided lug head and will make you think of the key used to tighten roller skates.

When you tighten the skins, try to get equal tension all around the drum head. This will keep the drum in tune, and it will produce a more even sound.

The Bass Drum

Years ago, the bass drums were much larger and certainly more awkward to carry around than they are today. Modern drums are generally smaller and easier to handle. The average bass drum is 14 inches deep and 20 or 22 inches in circumference.

The skins of the bass drum are fastened to the shell of the drum in the same manner as those of the snare drum. The difference is that the rods which loosen or tighten the skins can usually be manipulated by hand. No key is needed. The degree of tightness or looseness depends upon the drummer. You experiment with different tensions to find the sound you prefer.

Until a few years ago drum heads were made from calfskin. An important change came when plastic was molded into drum heads. This is an improvement because calfskin was easily affected by humidity. When the air was moist, the drummer had to tighten his skins periodically to keep a "crisp" sound. But with plastic heads, the drummer rarely has to tighten his heads after initial tuning because they are hardly affected by changes in humidity.

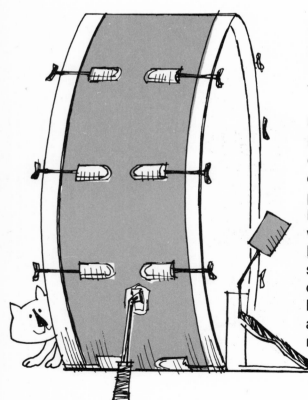

The Tom-toms

Two different tom-toms are generally used by drummers. The first is the small tom-tom, mounted on the bass drum. The other is the large tom-tom, which is placed on the floor to the right of the snare drum. The floor tom-tom has adjustable legs, and it can be raised or lowered to the height most comfortable for you. Since it is larger, it naturally has a deeper sound than the small tom-tom.

The snare drum and the bass drum have two drum heads, one on the top and one on the bottom. You may have noticed, however, that many rock drummers use a bass drum and tom-toms that do not have a bottom head. These have a sound the drummers like.

The tom-toms are the least necessary of all drums. Unless you are a solo artist and know how to use these drums they are more for show than practical use. Until you are further along in your development as a drummer you don't need tom-toms. They take up a lot of room and won't be necessary for use with this book. Everything you learn will only require a bass drum, snare drum, and cymbals.

Cymbals

Some drummers use an array of cymbals of different sizes. These are mounted on stands or holders around the drum set. For now you will only need one large "ride" cymbal, which can be mounted to a holder on the bass drum. This cymbal should be 18 or 20 inches in diameter.

The hi-hat, a set of two cymbals, is sometimes referred to as the "sock" cymbals. The hi-hat is usually placed to the left of the snare drum, where it is played with the left foot. When the foot presses down on the pedal, the two cymbals come together to make a "chick" sound.

The average hi-hats are 13 or 14 inches in diameter. They may, of course, be larger if the player prefers. The hi-hat can usually be taken apart so that it folds up and fits nicely into a special case which also holds the snare drum and its accessories.

If you have a hi-hat, spend some time taking it apart and then putting it together. You'll understand after this how it is made and how it works.

SETTING UP YOUR DRUM SET

Now that you know the names of the parts of your drum set it's time to learn how to set them up.

First, place the bass drum on the floor. Attach the spurs to each side of the front rim. The spurs will stop the round bass drum from rolling over the floor.

Now attach the foot pedal to the rim of the bass drum. The pedal has a little round beater which strikes the skin of the bass when the pedal is pushed down with your right foot. (Remember, I am assuming you are a righty. If not, you should play the opposite hand or foot and set up the drums in the reverse of the position described here.)

Hook the long cymbal holder to the right side of the bass drum shell. There is probably a piece of metal built into the drum through which the holder slides. If you find nothing on your bass drum to grasp the holder, there are cymbal holders that can be mounted on the bass or will stand on the floor. Once the holder is firmly attached, place the large ride cymbal on the top of the holder.

Open the snare drum stand and place the snare on it, then push it close to the bass drum, a little to the left of the foot pedal. The hi-hat (sock cymbals) is placed to the left of the snare drum and played with the left foot.

There you have it—the basic setup. The tom-toms are not necessary, but if you do have them, just place the large one on the floor to your right. Then mount the small one on the bass.

Meet the Drumsticks

There are several different ways to hold the drumsticks, as you probably know from watching drummers. Here, however, I will only show you one way, the "matched grip." It is the most natural of all ways to hold the sticks. In fact, the playing of most percussion instruments requires this grip.

The basic grip is exactly the same in each hand. Hold the drumstick between your thumb and index finger.

Now, place the remaining three fingers under and around the stick. Your palms should be facing down. When you play, try to move only your wrists. Keep your arms as steady as possible.

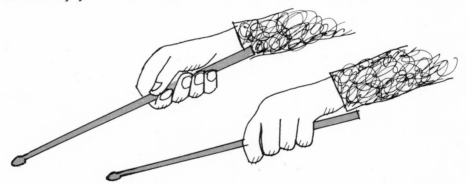

Now that you have the drums set up in the proper position and know how to hold the sticks, have a seat. There are special drum stools you can adjust to your height. If you do not have one, sit on a chair or regular stool. You can use a pillow if you feel you have to sit higher. It will also make you more comfortable.

The snare stand and cymbal holder are adjustable. You can move them up or down until you find a comfortable height for them in relation to how you're sitting.

Place your right foot on the bass drum pedal and your left foot on the hi-hat pedal. Pick up a pair of sticks and play. That's right: PLAY! You've been reading long enough. Hit anything you want to. Make as much noise as you can!

Good! You've gotten rid of some frustrations and can get down to the business of learning how to apply the beats you have learned at the drum set. By the way, banging at the drums is an excellent way to get rid of aggressive feelings. When I'm mad, I often find myself going to the drums and practicing—very LOUD.

Note: Drumsticks come in many different sizes. When buying a pair, simply find two sticks that seem to be comfortable in your hands. Try to see to it that they're of equal length and weight. This will help to produce an even sound as you play. If and when you get a private instructor, he or she will probably give you more specific advice as to what sticks to purchase. Many teachers like to start their students out with a 5A or 2B stick. You might start by asking for sticks with those numbers and see how you like them. The numbers refer to the sizes of the sticks.

BASIC BEATS AT THE DRUM SET

You learned six basic beats by tapping your right hand on your right thigh, your left hand on your left thigh, and your feet on the floor.

Now you will actually play the beats you have learned at a set of drums. And you'll be playing with sticks instead of your hands. The coordination involved is precisely the same. Simply follow these directions:

1. Always strike your right stick against the large ride cymbal.
2. Always strike your left stick against the snare drum.
3. Play your bass drum with your right foot, and your hi-hat with your left foot.

That's all there is to it.

The Waltz

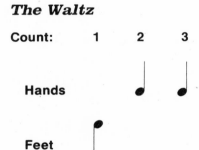

Remember, play both feet together only on the count of 1. Play both hands together only on the counts of 2 and 3.

Repeat the beat until you can play it without any hesitation. Your strainers at the bottom of the snare drum should be "on." In other words, they should be tight against the bottom skin in order to produce the distinctive snare sound.

The Lindy

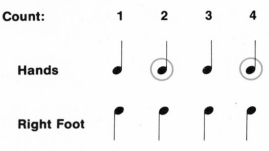

Count:	1	2	3	4
Hands	♩	Ⓞ	♩	Ⓞ
Right Foot	♩	♩	♩	♩

Remember, your right hand and your right foot play at the same time on the counts of 1, 2, 3, 4 while your left hand strikes the snare drum only on the counts of 2 and 4, the circled notes. If possible, play your left foot together with your left hand on the counts of 2 and 4.

Keep the strainers at the bottom of the snare drum right against the bottom skin, in the "on" position.

If you want to play softer, you can use brushes instead of sticks. These are made of thin strands of wire held in a long sheath. You simply slide them out of their sheath and use them the same way you do the sticks. The sound, however, is much softer than that made by sticks. You might use the brushes for the Waltz, Lindy, and Fox-trot. But you wouldn't use brushes in playing the basic Rock beat.

The Rock Beat

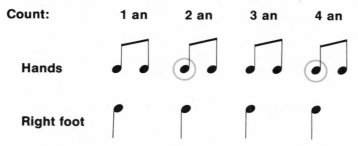

Count: 1 an   2 an   3 an   4 an

Hands

Right foot

Remember, the right hand will be playing steady eighth-notes on the ride cymbal while the left hand strikes the snare drum only on the counts of 2 and 4 (the circled notes).

The right foot will play the bass on the counts of 1, 2, 3, 4, and if possible, the left foot will play the hi-hat on the counts of 2 and 4.

While playing rock, the snares remain in the "on" position. If, however, you use this beat for the Rhumba or Cha-cha, be certain to lower the strainers away from the bottom skin. This means keeping the switch in the "off" position, thereby producing a tom-tom sound from the snare.

RUDIMENTS: EXERCISES TO DEVELOP TECHNIQUE

One important aspect of learning to play drums is the development of **technique.** By technique I mean speed, control, endurance, sensitivity of touch, and evenness of sound.

The development of technique is a long and difficult process. It usually takes many years of serious practice before a musician reaches a high degree of control over his instrument. Certain exercises have always been used to help the drummer in the development of such a technique. These exercises are known as **rudiments.**

There are 26 rudiments in all. Since a book like this can only help you so far, I have selected some of these rudiments for you to learn in a modified form. The ones I've selected are the most practical ones for your present needs.

Each rudiment is to be practiced slowly at first. You must see that an even sound is produced. This means the same volume of sound is made by each stick. One way to do this is to lift each stick to the same height. When you lift one stick higher than the other, that stick tends to produce a louder sound.

After you have practiced a rudiment at a slow tempo, try to increase the speed gradually. Your goal is to play each rudiment as smoothly and evenly as possible, at an increasingly faster tempo.

Important: Never lose control and evenness as you try for speed. Only increase speed when you feel you have gained control of the rudiment at a slower tempo.

You will notice that for each rudiment the fingering, or "sticking," is written out. This means you are told which hand to play for each note.

A written count is given above each note. You must be certain to count out loud. There is no mention of using feet. The rudiments are basically designed to develop technical ability with the hands. If you wish, you may try to substitute feet in place of hands to gain this experience, but this is not at all necessary.

Try to memorize each rudiment so that you can play it without looking at the music. Remember: slow and constant practice will eventually bring success.

Rudiments: Ruffs and Rolls

Three Stroke Ruff
Count:

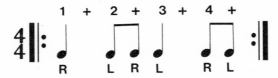

The two dots at the beginning and end of the exercise mean that you must repeat the exercise one more time. For now, however, keep repeating the exercise over and over until it can be played smoothly, without hesitation.

Four Stroke Ruff
Count:

The symbol ⸆ is called a quarter-rest. In this case, you should not play anything for one beat but simply count as shown.

36

Five Stroke Ruff
Count:

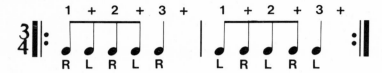

Five Stroke Roll
Notice that the difference between a Five Stroke ruff and the Five Stroke roll is in the fingering. A ruff is made up of single alternating strokes, R L R L. A roll is made up of double strokes, two on each hand, R R L L.

Count:

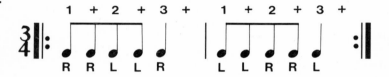

Seven Stroke Ruff
Count:

Seven Stroke Roll
Count:

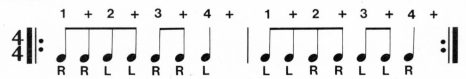

Nine Stroke Ruff
Count:

R L R L R L R L R   L R L R L R L R L

Nine Stroke Roll
Count:

R R L L R R L L R   L L R R L L R R L

Rudiments: Paradiddles

All of the rudiments you have just been practicing are made up of either single or double strokes. The rudiments which follow are a combination of single and double strokes. They fall in the category called *Paradiddles.*

Remember to play these paradiddles slowly at first, then gradually increase the tempo. Do not play the foot. Be sure to count out loud.

Single Paradiddle
Count:

R L R R L R L L

Double Paradiddle

Count:

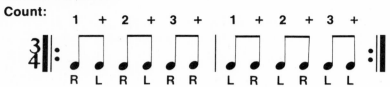

Triple Paradiddle

Count:

The Long Roll

One of the most difficult techniques for a drummer to master is the Long Roll. It is considered a rudiment and is, in fact, an extension of the Five, Seven, and Nine Stroke rolls. The difference is that the drummer does not end the double strokes on the fifth, seventh, or ninth beat. He simply keeps playing the double strokes until it's appropriate to end according to the music.

There are two ways to learn the Long Roll. The first is a very rudimental and traditional approach. The player starts slowly at first, keeping wrists and hands as relaxed as possible. Two strokes are played on each hand and, gradually, the speed is increased. As you gain the ability to play faster and faster (keeping two distinct strokes on each hand), the double strokes begin to sound somewhat like a machine gun. This is the kind of roll that is played by drummers in a marching band.

A rudimental approach to the Long Roll takes several years to develop. The slow process, however, brings the player many benefits in the form of speed and control.

There is a second approach to learning to roll. It is known as the "Press Roll" or "Buzz Roll" approach. Here the player does not play two distinct notes with each hand. Instead, as each stick hits the drum head it is allowed to press or "buzz" against the skin. It is difficult to tell precisely how many times the stick actually rebounds against the skin, but it is usually more than twice.

As you alternately "buzz" each stick against the skin rapidly the sound of a roll gradually emerges.

40

Try applying this approach and you should be able to produce a rolling sound in a fairly short time. Actually say "buzz" as you strike each stick against the skin and allow it to rebound.

Note: You will find the roll is indicated by three short lines across the stem of the note.

The Buzz Roll approach does not produce a roll with a very even sound at first. But faithful practice will in time improve the sound.

You should spend some time on each approach to the roll. At least five to ten minutes a day is what I recommend. Remember that the rudimental approach is excellent for developing speed and control in your hands. The Buzz Roll approach will have you playing the roll in a shorter time and is, in fact, the roll used most often by drummers in a symphony orchestra and dance band.

Special Accent Study

An accented note is one that is played louder than the other notes in a measure. It is common to see accented notes in music. They're indicated with a little arrow head ($>$) above or below the notes.

The next fifteen exercises will develop your ability to play accents. Such an ability will give you added strength and control of your hands. You should play each exercise slowly, accenting only the accented notes. Practice each exercise over and over many times before going on to the next.

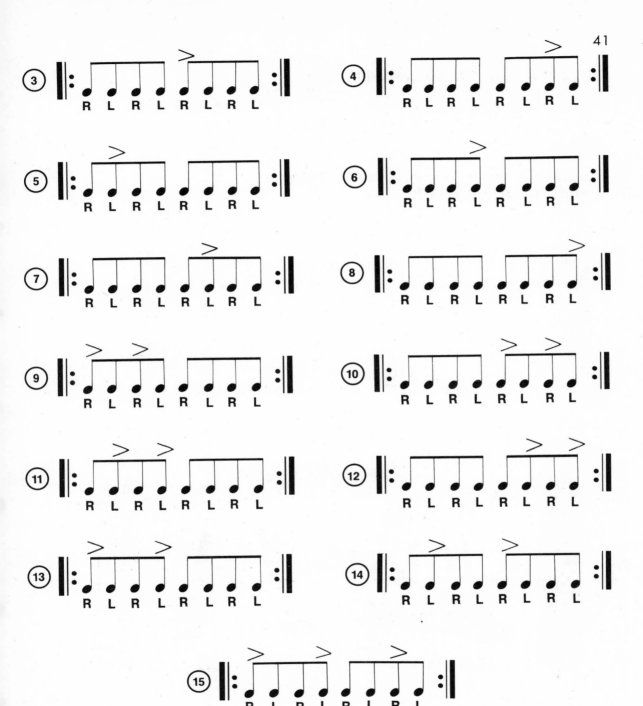

QUESTIONS AND ANSWERS

Some questions about playing drums are asked over and over. Here's the way I answer them based on my experience as a drummer and teacher.

What is the difference between a drummer and a percussionist?

In the percussion family of instruments are the nonpitched instruments such as the drums and a whole host of small rhythm instruments: maraca, tambourine, cowbell, and so on. Also included in the percussion family are certain instruments with pitch: timpani (a set of two or three kettledrums), xylophone, marimba, and vibraphone, as well as some others.

The term "percussionist" therefore refers to a person who can play all the instruments in the percussion family. The term "drummer," however, usually means a person who can play the drum set—that is to say, the nonpitched instruments. That person may or may not be able to play the pitched instruments of the percussion family.

Can I study in school without going to a
private drum instructor?

Yes, you can, but I don't recommend it and I will explain why.

First, school lessons are often for groups. If possible, I suggest you have private instruction.

Also, teachers certified to teach in a public school are usually band directors, able to teach several instruments at a beginning level. While a few band directors begin as percussion players, their first instrument is more commonly in the string, woodwind, or brass family. No one can be an expert at every instrument because each instrument takes years of study. The teacher in your school, if he or she is not a percussion player, may know many of the fundamentals of drumming. But the chances are that he or she is limited in full knowledge of drums. So, if you can afford it, I would recommend going to a private teacher who specializes in percussion.

Where do I go to find a teacher, and how much
do lessons cost?

There are many places where you can go to learn drums. One of the simplest ways is to turn to listings in your classified telephone book. Look under *Music Instruction,* where the names of private drum teachers may be listed.

Many music stores offer drum instruction. These stores, too, are listed in the classified directory. One good way to be likely to get a quality instructor is to contact a music store that deals only in percussion equipment. If you live in a large city, there's usually one store specializing in drums. The owner will probably know the really fine teachers in town and will be happy to recommend someone.

Another way to find a teacher is to phone the music department of a college in your area. Ask for the percussion instructor. Many of the people who teach percussion in college also teach drums privately.

You might speak to the band director in your junior high or high school. Professional music teachers usually know one another, and you should have little trouble in finding someone.

The cost of lessons varies greatly. If you want a teacher to come to your home it will probably cost more than if you go to the teacher's music studio. I hesitate to quote figures, but I probably won't be too far off if I say that the cost of private instruction is on the average between $5 and $15 a lesson.

Most students take one lesson a week. I suggest that if a teacher asks more than you can afford, you talk it over together. Perhaps you can take a shorter lesson or one lesson every other week. Don't be afraid to ask—teachers are often very interested in developing good students. Teaching music is not just a business with them and they may be willing to make some arrangement for you.

How long does it take to learn to play the drums?
This is probably the one question asked by everyone first beginning to study the instrument. There are, unfortunately, no definite answers. Everything depends upon the talent of the individual together with the amount of time spent in practice. If you are thinking of becoming a professional musician, many years of training are required, with hours and hours of practice each day.

Suppose you are simply interested in the drums as a hobby.

You just want to "keep time" in order to play some basic beats with a little band. You can learn to do this in a matter of weeks.

How long should I practice each day?

In the beginning, an hour a day is generally enough time to practice a lesson. There will always be certain lessons which require more effort than others. Some students, and indeed some professionals, practice between three and eight hours each and every day. This is unnecessary, of course, if you're thinking of playing the drums only as a hobby.

Practicing shouldn't get in the way of enjoying yourself in other ways with your friends, and it should never interfere with your school work. If you arrive at the point where you decide to become a professional musician, then you have to forget about the clock and practice for as long as it takes to develop the necessary skills.

Do girls study drums?

In the past, it was more common to see a girl playing the piano or a stringed instrument than a brass, woodwind, or percussion instrument. Perhaps drums seemed unladylike, but all that is changing. Although girls are still in the minority so far as the overall number of drum students is concerned, almost any experienced teacher will tell you that the number of girls coming

to study the drums is definitely on the increase. And while there aren't many women drummers playing professionally, they have achieved a high status in just about every field of percussion, from classical music to jazz and rock. So if you're a girl, you can feel perfectly at ease in learning the drums—there are thousands more like you across the country.

How can I tell if I have talent?

It's often said that it takes 99 per cent sweat and 1 per cent talent to become a good musician, and I tend to agree with that. People need very little basic talent to develop into good musicians, and most of us possess that basic amount. The difference between students lies not so much in their talent as in their interest and desire to learn.

Some students do not show their talent until many years after they've begun to study. Others seem to have a great deal of talent but never progress as far as one might have expected of them.

Actually, you shouldn't concern yourself with the question of talent but simply with whether the instrument interests you. If so, that's reason enough to study and practice. When you do that, you are certain to achieve a degree of competence.

How can I practice if I live in an apartment house?

Almost anyone who lives in an apartment house and studies an instrument has a problem. Or perhaps it would be more correct to say that the neighbors have a problem. It's not easy to listen to a beginner practicing on an instrument, especially if it is for hours on end.

As I mentioned earlier, drummers do have practice pads which cut down on much of the sound. Still, the tapping sound even on a practice pad often penetrates walls and floors. You might do well to be straightforward with your neighbors. Tell them that you are learning the drums and that you will try not to disturb them. This direct approach usually works very well. No one wants to prevent a person from learning, and perhaps a time can be worked out when your practicing will not bother anyone. But when it comes to playing on the drum set, this may hardly be possible. You may have to forget about playing on the set during the week and simply play for an hour or two during the middle of the day on weekends. Again, try to work it out with your neighbors.

Although I keep mentioning neighbors, parents sometimes can't stand the "banging" and are often more of a problem than anyone else. There's an old joke that says the first thing a child learns when he gets a drum set for a present is that he'll never get another one!

Once I've mastered the contents of this book, how can I join or organize a band?

One way to form a little group is to look up the name of a guitar or accordian teacher in the classified telephone directory. Call and explain you're interested in forming a little band. Ask if there are students who might be interested in joining. Usually the teacher will recommend someone your own age who lives nearby. If one teacher cannot help you, try another.

If you go to junior high or high school, speak to your band director. You might also post a message on the school bulletin board or put an ad in the school newspaper, asking anyone interested to contact you.

Is it easy to become a professional drummer, and can a person make a good living as a musician?

To answer honestly, I have to say that the outlook is not particularly good. In most places there are many more drummers than there are jobs, and this situation is likely to grow worse.

Some people feel that there's always room for a really great drummer, and perhaps that's true. But becoming a great drummer requires years of hard practice along with a high degree of talent. In answering another question, I mentioned that most people have enough talent to become good musicians, but becoming a great one is another story.

You can practice hard, go to college, and study music education with your major instrument being percussion. Upon graduation you might teach music in school, but that is a far-off goal. Before you think about becoming a professional, start by studying and playing. After a few years you'll be in a better position to think about a professional career. You can discuss it with your teacher and consider the advice you're given about the opportunities available at that time.

Who are some of the great drummers I can hear?

There are so many that it's really impossible to name them all. Many of the great drummers are not even known to the public. Besides, there are drummers who are only great in one area of performance. A great jazz drummer, for instance, may not necessarily be a great rock player. A great timpanist with a symphony orchestra may not play jazz very well.

Most of the drummers who have recorded with bands are fine players, and it's worthwhile listening to as many drummers as possible, whether they're "great" or simply very good.